Shhh!

UNLOCKING THE SECRETS OF THE FORTUNE 1000'S BUSINESS PLAYBOOK

SUCCESS TACTICS FOR SMALL BUSINESSES TO ENGAGE TOP CORPORATIONS

ALICE GORDON HOLLOWAY, PH.D.

www.TrueVinePublishing.org

Secrets of the Fortune 1000s' Business Playbook
Alice Gordon Holloway, Ph.D.

Published by
True Vine Publishing Co.
810 Dominican Dr.
Nashville, TN 37228
www.TrueVinePublishing.org

ISBN: 978-1-962783-81-1 Paperback

DEDICATION

I extend my deepest gratitude to my husband Weymon, for giving me the encouragement and space to bring this book to life. To my children and family, who have been invaluable and helped to shape my journey in countless ways.

And to my readers—thank you for allowing my words to become a part of your world.

I dedicate this book to my mother who will always be remembered... Beatrice "BK" Gordon Ferguson.

TABLE CONTENTS

PURPOSE OF THE GUIDE

Welcome to the essential guide for entrepreneurs seeking to unlock the secrets that Fortune 1000 corporations use to dominate their industries. Whether you're a seasoned business owner or launching your first enterprise, this book offers success business insights, strategies, and practical steps designed to propel your business to new heights. My goal for writing this book is to help entrepreneurs, business leaders and practitioners to successfully engage in building successful ecosystems, networks, business growth by using concepts I have outlined to grow strategically using solid, proven business tactics that can immediately be implemented.

Building upon countless interactions, I have learned that successful entrepreneurial founders and leaders continually conduct what I call the "5 Rs" Audit - Review, Re-evaluate, Refine, Re-measure, and even Re-invent themselves and their companies. Over the past years, I have opened multiple business entities and continually experience the 5 R's as the essential tapestry where entrepreneurial founders can build, uncover and unlock the secret playbook that Fortune 1000 corporations use to dominate their respective business enterprise and industries.

I wrote this guide from my perspective of leading and managing within a publicly traded corporate utility company, supply chain and supplier vendor manager and Award-Winning business strategist and developer with years of experience supporting numerous entities as a corporate strategist with direct touchpoint to business executives. Now I seek to learn and share entrepreneurial strategies and uncover the knowledge contained herein which I have distilled into actionable advice that anyone can apply.

IMPORTANCE OF LEARNING FROM FORTUNE 1000 CORPORATIONS

Fortune 1000 companies have perfected the art of business success through years of experience, innovation, and strategic planning. Their achievements are no accident and in many cases has stood the test of time. By understanding and emulating their practices, you can bypass common pitfalls and accelerate your journey to success. This guide aims to demystify the strategies these corporations employ, providing you with the tools to build and grow your business effectively.

Each chapter is designed to be a self-contained module, offering deep dives into specific aspects of business success. Feel free to read sequentially or jump to the chapters which address your most pressing needs.

Take notes and time to reflect at the end the chapter. Each section concludes with actionable steps to help you implement the concepts discussed, ensuring that you can translate knowledge into tangible results right away.

Onward and upward…!

"MY MISSION IN LIFE IS NOT
MERELY TO SURVIVE, BUT TO
THRIVE; AND TO DO
SO WITH SOME PASSION, SOME
COMPASSION, SOME HUMOR,
AND SOME
STYLE."
— MAYA ANGELOU

OPENING

UNVEILING THE SECRETS OF CORPORATE AMERICA

In the summer of 2018, I had been invited to serve as the guest speaker at a vendor and business conference hosted by Nissan Corporation, a national automotive leader and manufacturer. At the time, I was not entirely certain of the session's ultimate goal —I only knew that my expertise had been requested, and I needed to prepare to deliver. However, as I prepared for the engagement, I realized that this was more than just another speaking opportunity. It was a chance to bridge the gap between corporate giants and the small businesses striving to work with them. The event took place in the small town of Itta Bena, Mississippi, a city with a unique name and rather fitting backdrop for such an important conversation.

As I prepared for my presentation, I faced a critical question; "How could I provide value beyond what the business community had already heard? I knew I had to deliver a message that was truly insightful, something that went beyond conventional wisdom. As I walked into the venue where I was to present for 75-minutes, I could not ignore the weight of the moment but three pressing questions gnawed at me and swirled in my mind – such as –

Have they heard all of this before?

Will the audience connect with my message?

Am I truly prepared to reveal what corporations never openly share with small businesses?

These doubts fueled my determination and desire to connect with the audience in a meaningful, sincere and impactful way. My presentation focused on the unspoken truths of corporate partnerships—the hidden dynamics, unpublicized strategies, and the nuances that can make or break a small business trying to scale within the supply chains of major enterprises. I was invited not to simply present a canned boring speech, I was there to leave an impact—on Nissan, on its vendors, suppliers and on my-self. Then, the moment arrived.

As I reflected on the quote about perseverance, I had heard many times before, "you miss 100% of the shots you don't take", I pondered this taking a deep labored breath. A Nissan executive turned to me and said, "Alice, you're up next, we're looking forward to your presentation." This was it, MY shot.

As I took the stage, I realized that my corporate and entrepreneurial journeys had led me to this exact point. I was intentional and wanted to ensure the business-based audience walked away with valuable business nuggets and knowledge that could transform their trajectory. The answer was clear, I had to spill the tea. In 2018, I had finally decided to share and pull back the curtain on what large corporations don't tell small businesses—the real strategies, the unspoken rules, the competitive advan-tages hidden in plain sight. These insights, often guarded within corporate circles, are precisely what small businesses need to level the playing field and scale with confidence.

This moment was more than a speech, it was the spark that ignited my journey to write this book. If you're reading this, you now have access to those same game-changing insights. I contemplated. I labored. I procrastinated and now it is here.

If you are reading this book, you now know the per-ilous impetus for why I began this journey in 2018.

Welcome to my new book, **_Shhhy! Unlocking the Secrets of the Fortune 1000's Business Playbook - Success Tactics for Small Business to Engage Top Corporations_** a guide to the hidden rules of corporate success and how small businesses can break through. This book refines my story to share business insights, value-driven approaches coupled with industry relevance. Happy reading!

THE VISION

CHAPTER 1

SUCCESS FORMULA: UNDERSTANDING THE BASICS OF SUCCESS IN BUSINESS

"I've learned that you shouldn't go through life with a catcher's mitt on both hands; you need to be able to throw some things back."

— *Maya Angelou*

CHAPTER 1:

SUCCESS FORMULA
UNDERSTANDING THE BASICS
OF SUCCESS IN BUSINESS

W ould you agree that success in business is not a matter of luck or chance but rather a bit of pixie dust, grit and chewing gum? It is also the result of a well-formulated strategy, relentless execution, and the ability to adapt and innovate. Fortune 1000 companies thrive because they understand the key components that drive success and continuously refine their approaches to stay ahead of the competition. I have identified key components to launch, sustain and scale a business onto the road to success in the world of commerce.

KEY COMPONENTS OF A SUCCESSFUL BUSINESS ACTION-BASED STRATEGY

VISION AND MISSION:
A clear vision and mission provide direction and purpose. They inspire and align the efforts of everyone in the organization towards common goals.

Strategic Planning: Effective strategic planning involves setting long-term goals, identifying the steps needed to achieve them, and allocating resources appropriately. It's about making informed decisions and preparing for the future.

Market Understanding: Deep knowledge of the market, including customer needs, industry trends, and competitive landscape, is crucial. This allows businesses to identify opportunities and threats, positioning themselves advantageously.

Foster Innovation and Adaptation: Staying relevant requires constant innovation. Whether it's through product development, process improvements, or business model adjustments, the ability to adapt to changing conditions is vital. Encourage creativity and experimentation within your organization. Allocate resources for research and development (R&D) and be open to new ideas.

Optimize Operations: Streamline your processes to increase efficiency. Look for ways to reduce waste, improve quality, Efficient operations minimize waste and maximize productivity. Take your time because this aspect includes everything from vendors who supply product and services, your various customer segments, supply chain as well as your employees and part-time or fulltime contractors.

Manage Finances Wisely: Keep a close eye on your financial health. Regularly review your budgets, monitor cash flow, and make data-driven financial decisions. Sound financial management ensures that your business remains solvent and profitable. This involves budgeting, forecasting, and reviewing your numbers early and often.

Here are two examples from two well-known companies, Apple and Amazon. Amazingly, both companies are ubiquitous and are known around the world by one name. Apple's success can be attributed to its relentless focus on innovation, exceptional product design, and a deep understanding of consumer desires. Their strategic plan-ning and marketing prowess have set them apart as in-dustry leaders. In comparison, Amazon's success is built on operational excellence and customer obsession. Both companies have made strategic investments in technol-ogy and infrastructure have enabled them to scale rapidly and dominate the e-commerce space. You can adopt some of these key focal points as you build and scale your business enterprise.

As outlined the six steps above helps to provide a north star that can begin to set the company on a growth path in the beginning.

SUMMARY The success formula of Fortune 1000 companies is built on a foundation of clear vision, strategic planning and market understanding, innovation, operational excellence, and financial acumen. By adopting these principles and tailoring them to your unique business context, you can set the stage for sustainable growth and long-term success in your emerging or large-scale business or corporation.

CHAPTER NOTES & REMINDERS
YOUR ACTIONABLE GOALS OR PLANS

1.	2.
3.	4.
5.	6.
7.	8.
9.	10.

ILLUSTRATIONS

CHAPTER 2

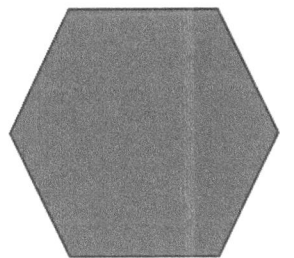

COMPETITION STRATEGIES

COMPETITION

COMPETITION STRATEGIES

A s a corporate executive with a PhD in business, I understand the intricacies and importance of sustaining a competitive advantage. This chapter will provide you with the insights and strategies needed to stay ahead of your competitors and ensure long-term success.

ANALYZING YOUR COMPETITORS

Understanding your competitors is the first step in developing effective competition strategies. This involves a commonly used comprehensive analysis tool which dates back to the 1960's created by Albert Humphrey, called the SWOT Analysis which represents Strengths, Weaknesses, Opportunities, and Threats (SWOT analysis).

Here's how to go about using this tool in your organization.

Identify Your Competitors: List your direct and indirect competitors. Direct competitors offer similar products or services, while indirect competitors provide alternative solutions to the same problem. You should understand both and know the difference.

Evaluate the Strengths and Weaknesses of Your Business and the Competition: Look at what your competitors do well and where they fall short. Take a detailed review of product offerings, customer service, marketing strategies, and how you operate vs. how they operate or entities you admire and would like to emulate.

Assess Their Market Position: Determine your com-petitors' market share, customer base, and growth trends. This will help you understand their influence and predict their future moves.

4.**Analyze Their Strategies**: Study their business mod-els, pricing strategies, marketing campaigns, and techno-logical advancements. Understanding their strategic choices will give you insights into their priorities and how they differentiate themselves.

Even as a budding entrepreneur in my first business, I was extremely curious and focused on enhancing my business' competitive advantage. That did not stop even as I transitioned to my corporate jobs. As faith would have it, I continued my quest while pursuing my PhD in business management to further investigate and answer the question of what does it take to develop and maintain a Competitive Advantage?

A competitive advantage is what sets your business apart and makes it more appealing to customers than your competitors. Here's how to develop and sustain the competitive advantage.

First, determine the Unique Value Proposition (UVP): Clearly define what makes your product or service unique. This could be superior quality, exceptional customer service, innovative features, or cost-effectiveness.

Secondarily, review the **customer focus** and really understand your customers' needs and preferences better than your competitors. Tailor your products and services to meet these needs and build strong relationships through personalized experiences.

Third, review **innovation**, this helps you to continuously innovate to stay ahead. This could be through new product development, process improvements, or adopting new technologies, its important and is what keeps your business engine churning for years to come.

Forth, focus on **operational efficiency**. Here is where optimization comes in to play in your operations to reduce costs and improve quality. Efficient processes can lead to faster delivery times, lower prices, and higher customer satisfaction. Embrace it.

Fifth, **develop your brand strength** Build a strong brand which resonates with your target audience. A powerful brand can create customer loyalty and make it difficult for competitors to lure your customers away.

Once you have developed a competitive advantage, the next phase is to implement strategies designed to leverage this advantage.

I offer five approaches below:

-Cost Leadership: Aim to be the lowest-cost producer in your industry. This allows you to offer lower prices or achieve higher margins.

-Be Different: Offer unique products or services that provide superior value, quality, features, and customer service.

-Focus on 1-2 Well Defined Goals: Target a specific market segment and tailor your offerings to meet the unique needs of this group. This can be achieved through cost focus or differentiation focus.

-Identify 1-2 Strategic Alliance Partners: You should not be on the lost island alone. Don't be afraid to partner with other businesses to leverage their strengths because this can provide access to new markets, technologies, and resources. Seek your other success partners to enhance your collective competitive advantage.

-Continuous Improve: Create a culture of continuous

improvement within your entity. Ask for feedback, lis-ten...YES, really listen and regularly review and refine your tactics to adapt to changing market conditions and stay ahead of competitors.

ACTIONABLE STEPS FOR ENTREPRENEURS

There are many of these steps that large corporations employ, I have distilled a few final actionable steps that you can implement in your enterprise.

Regularly analyze your competitors to understand their strengths, weaknesses, opportunities, and threats. Clearly articulate what makes your business unique and communicate this to your customers. Invest in under-standing your customers better. Use surveys, feedback, and market research to tailor your offerings. Allocate re-sources to research and development. Encourage creativity and experimentation within your team. Streamline your processes to improve efficiency. Look for ways to reduce costs and enhance quality. Build a Strong Brand that resonates with your target audience. Use consistent messaging and high-quality marketing materials.

Bottomline, implement and focus by choosing the strategy that best leverages your goals and implement it rigorously.

SUMMARY

Staying competitive in business requires a deep understanding of your competitors and a clear strategy differentiate your business. By taking a 30,000 feet elevated view, you can have a slight advantage with con-tinuous improvement and refinements which are key to staying ahead in a dynamic market.

This chapter provided you with a structured approach to understanding and out maneuvering your competitors. Implement these strategies diligently, and you'll be well on your way to enhancing your position.

CHAPTER NOTES & REMINDERS
YOUR ACTIONABLE GOALS OR PLANS

1.	2.
3.	4.
5.	6.
7.	8.
9.	10.

ILLUSTRATIONS

CHAPTER 3

4-CS OF THE RELATIONSHIP TOWER

RELATIONSHIPS

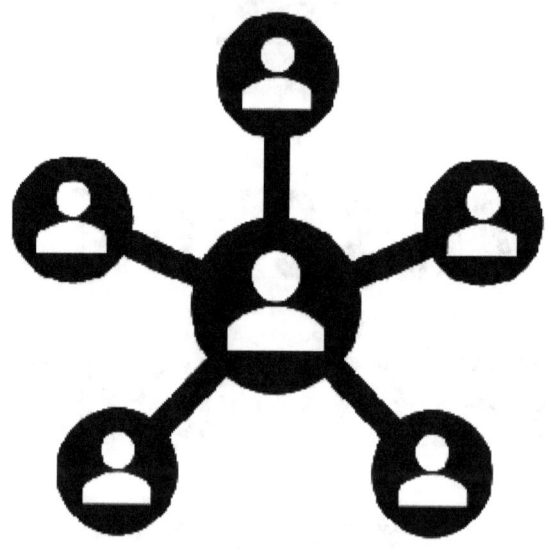

4-CS OF THE RELATIONSHIP TOWER

This is another big one, you might ask, what do *RELATIONSHIPS* have to do with it? Everything! Taking time to master the 4-Cs of the Relationship Tower — Communication, Collaboration, Commitment, and Consistency—can significantly enhance your business relationships, leading to sustained growth and success.

In this chapter, we will delve into each of these critical components, explore their contributions to strong re-lationships, provide practical applications, and outline actionable steps for entrepreneurs.

OVERVIEW OF THE 4-CS: COMMUNICATION, COLLABORATION, COMMITMENT, CONSISTENCY

COMMUNICATION

Effective communication is the foundation of all successful relationships. It involves the clear and concise exchange of information, ideas, and feedback between parties. In a business context, it ensures that all who are connected or slightly connected are aligned and informed which fosters trust and transparency.

COLLABORATION

◊ Collaboration is the act of working together towards a common goal. It leverages the strengths and skills of all participants to achieve better outcomes. In business, collaboration can drive innovation, improve problem-solving, and enhance productivity.

COMMITMENT

◊ Commitment refers to the dedication and loyalty that parties have towards each other and their shared goals. In a business relationship, it means being reliable, showing up, and putting in the effort to meet expectations and deliver results, not some of the time but every time.

CONSISTENCY

◊ Being consistent is critical. Large entities need to know they can count on you to do what you said you would do. It is about maintaining steady and reliable performance over time, which builds trust and credibility. Being predictable in your behavior, temperament and outcomes. In business, consistency in quality, service, and communication is key to sustaining relationships.

But how does each "C" contribute to strong relationships, let's take a deeper dive into my

4 C tower and begin with communications.

Communication builds trust: Trust is BIG. Open and honest communication fosters trust, as parties feel confident that they are being informed and heard. Don't slip in this area. Prevent mishaps and misunderstandings, thereby reducing the risk of misinterpretations and conflicts, ensuring that everyone is on the same page. This keeps peace and harmony on projects, processes and of course relationships. Do not forget that effective communication is essential for coordinating efforts and sharing knowledge, which enhances collaborative outcomes. Your goal should also be able to come back.

Collaboration helps to leverage diverse strengths. It is demonstrated time and time again that by working to-gether, businesses can leverage the unique strengths and expertise of their partners, leading to innovative solu-tions. Collaborative efforts often result in more comprehensive and effective problem-solving, as multiple perspectives are considered. Lastly, by implementing collaboration, the atmosphere fosters a sense of ownership and engagement which can contribute to shared success and increased opportunities and revenues.

Commitment ensures that parties can rely on each other to meet their obligations and deliver on promises. Demonstrating commitment builds long-term relationships, dedication and loyalty.

A strong commitment to each client, team and team mem-bers encourages mutual support, especially during chal-lenging times.

Finally, Consistent performance builds credibility and trust, as stakeholders know what to expect and can depend on reliable outcomes. It helps in demonstrating your service or product quality and delivery and en-hances customer satisfaction and loyalty.

HERE ARE 12 PRACTICAL APPLICATIONS FOR ANY BUSINESS OR LEADER TO CONSIDER:

1. Provide Regular Updates: Schedule regular updates with stakeholders to keep them informed about project progress and any changes.

2. Implement a Feedback Mechanisms: Implement feed-back mechanisms, such as surveys or suggestion boxes, to gather input and address concerns promptly.

3. Transparent Reporting: Use transparent reporting prac-tices to share performance metrics, financials, and other critical information.

4. Cross-Functional Teams: Form cross-functional teams to tackle complex projects, bringing together diverse ex-pertise and perspectives.

5. Partnerships: Establish strategic partnerships with other businesses to leverage complementary strengths and expand market reach.

6. Collaborative Tools: Utilize collaborative tools, such as project management software and communication plat-forms, to facilitate teamwork.

7. Build in Service Level Agreements (SLAs): Use SLAs to formalize commitments and ensure that expectations are clearly defined and met.

8. Implement Customer Loyalty Programs: Implement customer loyalty programs to reward and reinforce long-term relationships with clients.

9. Foster Virtual or In Person Employee Engagement: This can be forged among employees through engagement initiatives & recognition programs.

10. Standard Operating Procedures (SOPs): Develop and adhere to SOPs to ensure consistent quality and service delivery.

11. Quality Control: Implement rigorous quality control processes to maintain product & service standards.

12. Keep the Brand Consistent: Use brand guidelines to ensure consistency in marketing & communication efforts.

SUMMARY

The 4-Cs of the Relationship Tower—Communication, Collaboration, Commitment, and Consistency—are vital for building and sustaining strong business relationships. Through effective communication, you build trust and prevent misunderstandings. Collaboration leverages collective strengths and drives innovation. Commitment fosters reliability and long-term loyalty, while consistency builds credibility and ensures customer satisfaction.

By integrating these principles into your business practices, you can cultivate robust relationships that support your growth and success. Remember, the strength of your business relationships is a critical determinant of your overall success. Embrace the 4-Cs and watch your business thrive.

By understanding how each C contributes to relationship strength and implementing practical applications, entrepreneurs can enhance their business interactions and achieve long-term success. Consistent and dedicated efforts in these areas will build trust, foster loyalty, and drive collaborative innovation, ultimately leading to a competitive advantage for your organization or enterprise.

CHAPTER NOTES & REMINDERS
YOUR ACTIONABLE GOALS OR PLANS

1.	2.
3.	4.
5.	6.
7.	8.
9.	10.

ILLUSTRATIONS

CHAPTER 4

THE 5 A'HA MOMENTS: WHAT THE FORTUNE 1000'S WON'T TELL YOU

CONNECTING THE DOTS

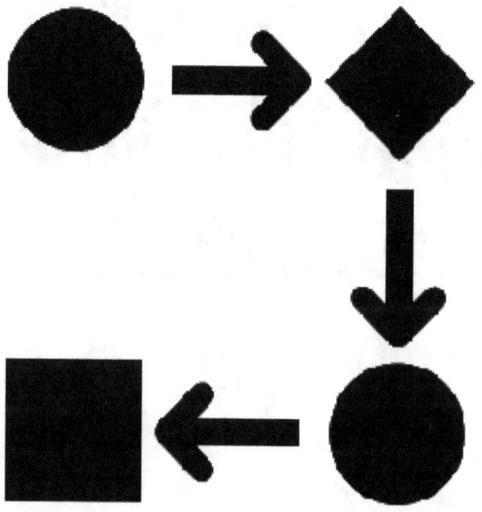

THE 5 A'HA MOMENTS:

WHAT THE FORTUNE 1000'S WON'T TELL YOU

N avigating the corporate landscape as a small business owner can be daunting, especially when dealing with Fortune 1000 companies. The stakes are high, and the rules of engagement are often unwritten. This section unveils the critical "A'HA Moments" that Fortune 1000 companies typically keep under wraps. Under-standing these insights will empower you to better prepare, strategize, and ultimately succeed in your business dealings with these corporate giants.

As a business college professor with a PhD, I've spent years studying the strategies and secrets of Fortune 1000 companies. These giants of industry have perfected their methods over decades, and while they are often tight-lipped about their inner workings, over the years, I have gained critical insights through interactions, inter-views and careful observation.

In this chapter, I'll share with you the A'HA moments that these corporations may not readily share but are crucial for understanding their modus operandi.

LARGE TOP CORPORATIONS HAVE MORE MONEY, ACCESS AND PATIENCE THAN YOU

The first A'HA moment is the realization that Fortune 1000 companies possess vast financial resources and a long-term perspective that small businesses often lack along with a significant amount of patience. This financial clout allows to these top companies to endure prolonged negotiations, invest heavily in R&D, and outlast smaller competitors in times of economic uncertainty.

Recognizing this disparity can help you strategize more effectively, ensuring you don't overstretch your resources. Large corporations can afford to play the long game, investing in projects and partnerships that may not yield immediate returns. Their deep pockets allow them to weather storms that could cripple smaller businesses. For entrepreneurs, this means understanding that while you may need quick wins to stay afloat, these large corporations are looking at long-term gains. Aligning your strategies to showcase not just immediate benefits but also long-term potential can make you more attractive.

2. THEY HAVE 6 OTHER BUSINESSES LINED UP WHO COULD TAKE YOUR SPOT

Competition is fierce, and Fortune 1000 companies usually have multiple vendors or partners vying for the same opportunity, attention and contracts. They operate in a competitive environment where options are abundant. This means that your position is never guaranteed, and there is always a risk of being replaced. Understanding this can drive you to continuously improve and innovate. Always be aware that your business needs to stand out and provide unique value to maintain your place in their ecosystem.

3. THEY ARE ALREADY SKEPTICAL & DISTRUSTING OF YOU

Leaders in large corporations tend to be cautious and skeptical when dealing with smaller businesses. This skepticism stems from concerns about reliability, scalability, and the ability to meet their stringent standards. To counter this, you must demonstrate credibility, deliver consistently, and build trust through transparent and proactive communication. Be prepared, they will scrutinize your business, your promises, and your track record.

To overcome this skepticism, you need to build credibility. This can be achieved through strong references, proven results, and a transparent approach that instills confidence in your ability to deliver.

4. THEY ARE HOLDING THEIR BREATH HOPING YOU CAN REALLY DELIVER ON WHAT YOU PROMISE

While Fortune 1000 companies can be complex, many of the internal leaders want you to succeed because it benefits them. They are essentially holding their breath, waiting to see if you can live up to your promises. This underscores the importance of under-promising and over-delivering. By managing expectations and consistently delivering exceptional results, you can turn this hopeful anticipation into trust and long-term partnerships.

5. YOU ARE SMALLER FISH AND THEIR REPUTATION IS ON THE LINE

The reputation of a Fortune 1000 company is a critical asset. Every interaction, partnership, and project they undertake reflects on their brand. This means that when they engage with your business, they are putting their reputation on the line.

Understanding this can help you appreciate the gravity of your interactions with these corporations. Conducting yourself with professionalism, integrity, and a focus on quality will help reinforce their decision to work with you and protect their reputation.

SUMMARY

Understanding these "A'HA Moments" is crucial for any small business aspiring to work with Fortune 1000 companies. Recognizing the vast financial resources and patience these giants possess, the intense competition for your spot, cautious optimism, and the impact of their reputation on every interaction is part of understanding the Playbook.

Armed with this knowledge, you can better navigate the complexities of these high-stakes business relationships and position your company for success.

CHAPTER NOTES & REMINDERS
YOUR ACTIONABLE GOALS OR PLANS

1.	2.
3.	4.
5.	6.
7.	8.
9.	10.

ILLUSTRATIONS

CHAPTER 5

KNOW THY NUMBERS :
8 CRITICAL BUSINESS
FUNDING FIGURES

THE NUMBERS

KNOW THY NUMBERS: 8 CRITICAL BUSINESS FUNDING FIGURES

T op 1000 Corporations Want You to Know These 8 Things. These companies operate with a set of core principles and metrics which guide their decision-making processes. Understanding these can provide you with a significant advantage in aligning your business strategies to meet their expectations.

In the highly competitive landscape of Fortune 1000 companies, there are specific key performance indicators (KPIs), objectives and key results (OKRs) and strategic considerations that these corporations prioritize. By understanding and integrating these into your business practices, you can better position yourself to engage with and appeal to these industry giants.

Here are the eight (8) crucial Financial revenue drivers that the top Corporations want you to know:

REVENUE STREAM

Fortune 1000 companies have diverse and robust

revenue streams. They are keenly interested in understanding how your business generates revenue and how stable and scalable these streams are. This includes examining your primary sources of income, secondary revenue streams, and any innovative approaches to monetization.

For entrepreneurs, it's essential to clearly articulate your revenue model. Ensure that it is well-documented and includes forecasts that demonstrate both current and future revenue potential. Transparency and reliability in your revenue streams will make your business more attractive to large corporations.

COST BENEFIT ANALYSIS

A thorough cost-benefit analysis (CBA) is a critical tool for decision-making in large corporations. They want to see that you understand the financial implications of your projects and can demonstrate a clear return on investment (ROI). This involves assessing the costs involved in a project and weighing them against the expected benefits.

Entrepreneurs should be prepared to present detailed CBAs for their proposals. Highlight how your solutions provide value that outweighs the costs and include both quantitative and qualitative benefits to make a compelling case.

RETURN ON INVESTMENT (ROI)

Return on Investment (ROI) is a key metric for Fortune 1000 companies. They need to see that their investments will yield significant returns. This means not only presenting a strong business case but also having a track record of delivering on your promises.

To appeal to these large entitics, be sure you can provide historical data and case studies that demonstrate high ROI. Show how your business strategies have previously translated into financial gains for your clients or partners.

GROSS PROFIT MARGIN

Understanding and optimizing gross profit margin is crucial for sustained profitability. Closely monitoring your Gross Profit Margin ensures that their operations are efficient and are generating sufficient profit from their revenue.

You should be able to clearly articulate your gross profit margins. The numbers matter. Focus on strategies you use to maximize this margin, such as cost control measures, pricing strategies, sustainable practices and operational efficiencies. A healthy gross profit margin indicates a strong and sustainable business model.

GROWTH STRATEGY

Fortune 1000 companies are constantly seeking growth opportunities, whether through market expansion, product innovation, or strategic acquisitions. They want to understand your growth strategy and how it aligns with their objectives.

Be prepared to discuss your short-term and long-term growth plans in detail. Highlight how you plan to scale your business, enter new markets, or innovate within your industry. Demonstrating a clear and achievable growth strategy will position you as a forward-thinking and dynamic partner.

MARKETING NICHE

Identify and highlights what makes your company unique. Own your narrative. Articulating your specialized marketing niche can be a significant competitive advantage. As an entrepreneur, you should emphasize your expertise in your specific market niche and provide insights into your market research, technology, experiences and customer segmentation. Demonstrate as often as you can how your niche strategy differentiates you from competi-tors and appeals to their specific customer needs.

SALES CYCLE/SALE PROCESS

A well-defined and efficient sales cycle is essential for driving revenue and managing customer relationships. Top companies are interested in how you manage your sales process from lead generation to closing deals.

Having a process is a sexy business tool to discuss. Outline your sales process, including the tools and tech-niques you use to manage leads, nurture prospects, and convert them into customers. Highlight any sales methodologies you employ and how you measure and optimize your sales peformance.

An optimized sales cycle im-proves conversion efficiency, while ratio analysis offers a comprehensive view of the company's financial health.

REAL – NOT PERCEIVED CAPABILITIES

Finally, Fortune 1000 company leaders need to un-derstand your core capabilities. This includes your techni-cal expertise, operational strengths, technological ad-vances and any unique competencies which set you apart from the competition. Provide a comprehensive overview of your capabilities, backed by examples and case studies. Demonstrate how your skills and resources align with the needs and goals of large companies. Showcasing your capabilities effectively will build confidence in your abil-ity to deliver high-quality results.

SUMMARY

Understanding these core business concepts and met-rics is essential for CEOs to drive their companies toward success. Possessing a handle on critical aspects large companies prioritize such as revenue streams, cost-benefit analysis, ROI, gross profit margin, growth strategy, marketing niche, sales cycle, and capabilities—entrepreneurs can better align their business strategies to meet the ex-pectations and standards of these industry leaders. By mastering these elements, leaders of smaller entities can make informed decisions which lead to sustained growth.

CHAPTER NOTES & REMINDERS
YOUR ACTIONABLE GOALS OR PLANS

1.	2.
3.	4.
5.	6.
7.	8.
9.	10.

ILLUSTRATIONS

THE CONNECTION

CHAPTER 6

INTENTIONAL RELATIONSHIP TACTICS

INTENTIONAL RELATIONSHIP TACTICS

I n the realm of entrepreneurship and business strategy, intentional relationship-building is not just an art; it's a strategic imperative. Whether you are a startup founder or a seasoned executive, the ability to cultivate and maintain meaningful connections can propel your business to new heights.

This chapter delves into specific tactics and strategies to foster intentional relationships that drive business success.

INTENTIONAL RELATIONSHIP TACTICS

DEVELOP COMMON GROUND

Finding common ground is the bedrock of any meaningful relationship. In a business context, this involves identifying shared interests, values, or goals with your counterparts. Whether it's a mutual interest in industry trends or a shared vision for community impact, establishing common ground sets the stage for a collaborative and productive relationship. This can be achieved through open conversations, active listening, and a genuine interest in the other party's perspectives and experiences.

IDENTIFY THE RELATIONSHIP BENEFITS

Every relationship should be mutually beneficial. As an entrepreneur, it's essential to identify and articulate the benefits that each party brings to the table. This could range from access to new networks, sharing of resources, or collaborative opportunities. By clearly understanding and communicating these benefits, you set a foundation for a relationship built on value and reciprocity.

COMMIT TO BUILDING A STRONG RAPPORT

Building rapport goes beyond surface-level interactions. It requires consistent and genuine efforts to connect on a deeper level. This involves regular communication, showing empathy, and being reliable. A strong rapport fosters trust and openness, making it easier to navigate challenges and seize opportunities together.

DEVELOP A TWO-WAY RELATIONSHIP

A two-way relationship is characterized by mutual respect, support, and contribution. It's important to ensure that the relationship is not one-sided. Both parties should feel valued and heard. This can be achieved through active engagement, providing constructive feedback, and celebrating each other's successes.

TOP 6 WAYS TO BUILD TRUSTING, EFFECTIVE RELATIONSHIPS

♦ **Build a Foundation First**

The foundation of a trusting relationship is built on transparency and authenticity. Start by being honest and straightforward in your interactions. Establishing a solid foundation of trust early on will make it easier to deepen the relationship over time.

♦ **Be Aware but Be Approachable**

Awareness of your surroundings and the dynamics at play in any interaction is crucial. However, it's equally important to remain approachable. Being open and friendly encourages others to engage with you, fostering a sense of community and collaboration.

Learn How to Survey the Room by Getting There Early

Arriving early to events or meetings gives you the opportunity to survey the room, understand the atmosphere, and identify key individuals to connect with. This proactive approach allows you to make informed decisions about who to engage with and how to approach them.

♦ **Be Prepared with a Solid Elevator Pitch**

A well-crafted elevator pitch is a powerful tool for making a strong first impression. Your pitch should succinctly convey who you are, what you do, and what you stand for. Include a humorous line which can help break the ice, and asking about the other person shows genuine interest in them. Try to listen effectively

♦ Watch Out for the "One Up" Move

In any relationship, it's important to avoid the temptation to "one-up" the other person. This behavior can undermine trust and create a competitive rather than collaborative atmosphere. Instead, focus on mutual growth and support.

♦ Be a Giver & Relationship Broker in Your Relationship – Go the Extra Mile

Adopting a giving mindset can significantly enhance your relationships. By going the extra mile and offering help without expecting anything in return, you demonstrate your commitment to the relationship and build goodwill.

MY 9 STEPS TO STRENGTHENING RELATIONSHIPS

1. KEEP THE LEAD WARM AND MAKE THE FOLLOW-UP CONNECTION QUICKLY

Timely follow-up is crucial in maintaining momentum in any relationship. Make it a habit to follow up promptly after initial meetings or interactions to keep the connection warm and show your interest.

2. LEARN AS MUCH AS YOU CAN ABOUT EVERYONE YOU WORK WITH

Understanding the people you work with on a personal and professional level can deepen your relationships. Take the time to learn about their interests, strengths, and challenges.

3. TREAT YOUR VENDORS/SUPPLIERS LIKE HONORARY EMPLOYEES

Vendors and suppliers are integral to your business operations. Treating them with the same respect and consideration as you would your employees fosters a collaborative and supportive environment.

4. LEARN EVERYONE'S BIRTHDAY

Remembering and acknowledging birthdays is a simple yet effective way to show you care. This small gesture can go a long way in building rapport and making people feel valued.

5. HAVE ONE-ON-ONE CONVERSATIONS WITH YOUR CUSTOMERS

Direct conversations with your customers can provide valuable insights into their needs and how you can better serve them. It also shows that you value their feedback and are committed to continuous improvement.

6. Contact Them Frequently but Don't Be a Pest

Regular communication is key to maintaining relationships, but it's important to strike a balance. Keep in touch frequently enough to stay connected, but not so much that you become a nuisance.

7. Acknowledge Good Work and Offer Compliments

Recognizing and appreciating the efforts of others can strengthen your relationships. Offering sincere compliments and acknowledging good work fosters a positive and supportive environment.

8. Be Flexible with the People You Can Count On

Flexibility and understanding are essential in maintaining strong relationships. Be willing to accommodate the needs and circumstances of those you can count on, and they will likely do the same for you.

9. Make Sure Employees Have Everything They Need to Do Their Jobs

Supporting your employees with the resources and tools they need to succeed demonstrates your commitment to their well-being and professional growth. This support can lead to increased loyalty and productivity.

SUMMARY

Intentional relationship-building is a critical component of business success. By developing common ground, identifying relationship benefits, committing to building rapport, and fostering two-way relationships, entrepreneurs can create a robust network of support and collaboration. Implementing the top ways to build trusting, effective relationships and following the steps to strengthen these connections will help ensure long-term success and growth.

CHAPTER NOTES & REMINDERS
YOUR ACTIONABLE GOALS OR PLANS

1.	2.
3.	4.
5.	6.
7.	8.
9.	10.

ILLUSTRATIONS

THE GLUE

CHAPTER 7

MOM THEORY

THE MOM THEORY

The MOM Theory revolves around three core principles: Maximize, Optimize, and Monetize

MAXIMIZE – UNCOVERING HIDDEN VALUE

This is the starting point for most businesses. To maximize is to expand your potential to the fullest. Whether it's maximizing revenue, customer satisfaction, or employee productivity, the focus is on getting as much value from every resource available. For an entrepreneur, this often

In business, the term "maximize" goes beyond merely increasing revenues. It's about uncovering untapped opportunities, whether through better resource allocation, partnerships, or market positioning. Most small businesses I've consulted with only scratch the surface of their potential. Maximization requires a deep dive into the existing value within your business.

ASK YOURSELF: ARE YOU FULLY UTILIZING YOUR CUSTOMER BASE?

Often, businesses focus on acquiring new customers but overlook opportunities to deepen relationships with existing ones. Existing clients are often willing to spend more if you provide more tailored, relevant solutions. –

ARE YOUR PROCESSES AS EFFICIENT AS THEY COULD BE?

Every dollar saved in operational efficiency is a dollar earned. Now let's examine how technology, automation, and streamlined workflows could free up resources. In my corporate experience, we constantly revisited how we could get more from our current assets before chasing after the next big thing.

For small businesses, maximizing isn't about adding more complexity but focusing on amplifying the core strengths you already possess.

OPTIMIZE

After maximizing, optimization is where efficiency comes into play. Optimization is about improving processes and reducing waste, whether in time, money, or resources. The goal is to achieve better results without increasing costs. As an entrepreneur, you may look at optimizing your operations through technology, refining workflows, or developing? Question everything.

How can you tweak your processes, your product, and your customer experience to create more value with less waste? When you optimize, you're fine-tuning what's already working. Think about this is relations to comparing this to professional athletes.

Successful athletes don't reinvent their training routine every season; instead, they make small adjustments that lead to incremental but compounding performance gains over time. You should do the same.

Another example is your pricing strategy. Is it optimized? When was the last time you reviewed or adjusted it to current market and economic conditions? Many entrepreneurs set prices and forget about them. However, pricing is dynamic. Your pricing should reflect the value you're offering and the market conditions.

Additionally, are you focused on the right metrics? Not all business metrics are created equal. In large corpo-rations, they constantly monitored key performance indicators (KPIs) that had a direct impact on growth. For you, these KPIs might include customer retention rates, profit margins, or sales cycles as I discussed earlier. Regularly evaluate whether you're tracking the right met-rics to guide your decision-making. Optimization is a continual process, and small improvements over time lead to significant gains. This is especially critical for entrepreneurs with limited resources. Efficiency is your best friend, and even marginal tweaks can create a competitive edge.

MONETIZE

Turning Value Into Profit (VIP) ultimately is the goal of every business - monetize value. If you're maximizing opportunities and optimizing operations, the next natural step is ensuring you're converting that value into PROFIT.

However, monetization doesn't happen in isolation—it's the result of a strategic interplay between maximization and optimization. Ask yourself are you leveraging multiple customers and revenue streams? One consideration is to diversify your revenue streams, introduce new products, services, or subscription models or lines or consider offering a license to your intellectual property perhaps.

When you have maximized and optimized, you should be creating value that customers are willing to pay a premium for. This means you can increase your margins without losing customers. Corporations do this all the time by bundling services, creating loyalty programs, and offering tiered pricing. Small businesses can do the same. Monetization is not about the immediate sale. It is about creating ongoing value so once you have made a sale, focus on providing enhanced value that keeps customers connected to you. Corporations invest heavily in customer lifetime value strategies, and small businesses must do the same to scale.

My MOM Theory is not a one-time tactic; it's a cyclical process. As an entrepreneur, you need to constantly revisit these three pillars: **Maximize, Optimize, and Monetize.**

You're always looking for hidden value, fine-tuning your approach, and ensuring that value turns into profits. The businesses that succeed in the long term understand that this is a continuous process, not a box to be checked off. By adopting my MOM Theory, you'll be thinking like a Fortune 1000 executive while operating with the agility and innovation that only small businesses can bring to the table.

THE KEY TAKEAWAY:

The MOM Theory is about alignment. When you maximize opportunities, optimize processes, and monetize value effectively, your business runs like a well -oiled machine. As you move forward, ask yourself: Are you ready to adopt the MOM mindset?

It's time to think bigger, act smarter, and build a business that lasts. --- This approach incorporates practical advice and strategic insight while keeping the language accessible to entrepreneurs.

'

CHAPTER NOTES & REMINDERS
YOUR ACTIONABLE GOALS OR PLANS

1.	2.
3.	4.
5.	6.
7.	8.
9.	10.

ILLUSTRATIONS

THE DEAL

CHAPTER 8

KILLERS AND DEAL BREAKERS

KILLERS AND DEAL BREAKERS

In the dynamic world of business, relationships are crucial for sustained success. However, certain behaviors and actions can severely damage or even destroy these valuable connections. This chapter focuses on identifying relationship killers, avoiding common deal breakers, and providing strategies for overcoming relationship issues. By understanding these pitfalls, entrepreneurs can foster stronger, more resilient relationships.

LIST OF RELATIONSHIP KILLERS

1. LACK OF COMMUNICATION

Poor communication is a significant relationship killer. Misunderstandings, unmet expectations, and conflicts often arise when communication breaks down. Regular, clear, and honest communication is essential to maintaining healthy business relationships.

2. INCONSISTENCY

Inconsistency in behavior, promises, or delivery can erode trust and reliability. Partners, clients, and employees need to know they can depend on you to follow through consistently.

3. LACK OF RESPECT

Disrespectful behavior, whether intentional or unintentional, can quickly sour relationships. This includes dismissive attitudes, ignoring contributions, or failing to acknowledge the value others bring.

4. SELFISHNESS

Focusing solely on your own needs and ignoring the needs of others can alienate partners and clients. Successful relationships require a balance of give and take.

5. NEGLECT

Failing to nurture and maintain relationships can lead to their deterioration. Regular check-ins, showing appreciation, and addressing concerns promptly are essential for keeping relationships strong.

5 TACTICS TO AVOIDING COMMON DEAL BREAKERS

1. ADDRESS UNMET EXPECTATIONS

Setting and managing expectations is crucial. Failing to meet agreed-upon terms or deliverables can be a major deal breaker. Always strive to under-promise and over-deliver.

2. BREACH OF TRUST

Trust is the foundation of any relationship. Breaches of trust, whether through dishonesty, lack of transparency, or unethical behavior, can be irreparable.

3. POOR CONFLICT RESOLUTION

Conflict is inevitable, but how it's handled can make or break a relationship. Avoiding conflicts, being defensive, or not seeking mutually beneficial solutions can escalate issues.

4. IGNORING FEEDBACK

Feedback is vital for growth and improvement. Ignoring or dismissing feedback from partners, clients, or employees can create frustration and hinder relationship development.

5. OVERPROMISING AND UNDERDELIVERING

Making promises that you cannot keep damages credibility. Be realistic about what you can achieve and communicate openly about any potential challenges.

MY LIST OF 10 ADDITIONAL KILLERS AND DEAL BREAKERS (SORRY, THERE ARE MANY)

TALKING EXCESSIVELY ABOUT YOURSELF

Constantly talking about yourself and your achievements can be a major turnoff in any conversation. It creates an impression of self-centeredness and can make the other person feel undervalued and ignored. Conversations should be balanced, with both parties having the opportunity to share and contribute. It's important to listen actively and show genuine interest in the other person's experiences and perspectives. Building a two-way dialogue fosters mutual respect and understanding, which are essential for strong relationships.

BORING THE OTHER PERSON

Learning when to put the brakes on is crucial in maintaining the other person's interest. Long-winded, monotonous talks can quickly bore your conversation partner, leading to disengagement. Pay attention to nonverbal cues, such as body language and facial expressions, to gauge their interest level. Engaging stories, relevant anecdotes, and timely pauses can help keep the conversation lively and engaging. Remember, an interesting conversation is often more about quality than quantity.

NOT BEING FOCUSED OR RELEVANT

Staying focused and relevant in conversations is essential for effective communication. Tangential or irrelevant topics can confuse and frustrate the other person.

Stick to the topic at hand and ensure your contributions add value to the discussion. Being concise and to the point demonstrates respect for the other person's time and keeps the conversation productive. Relevant and focused discussions help in building a clear and meaningful connection.

TALKING TOO LOUD OR TOO SOFT

Your volume can significantly impact how your message is received. Talking too loud can come across as aggressive or overbearing, while speaking too softly can be perceived as a lack of confidence or interest. Finding the right volume ensures that your message is conveyed clearly and respectfully. Adjust your volume based on the environment and the other person's preferences to maintain a comfortable and effective communication flow. A well-modulated voice helps in creating a pleasant conversational experience.

NOT GIVING FULL ATTENTION

Multitasking or being distracted during a conversation can signal disinterest and disrespect. Giving your full attention shows that you value the interaction and respect the other person. This involves maintaining eye contact, nodding, and responding appropriately to what they say. Avoiding distractions, such as checking your phone, helps in building a genuine connection. Full attention fosters trust and shows that you are fully engaged in the conversation.

BAD BREATH OR HYGIENE

Personal hygiene can have a significant impact on first impressions and ongoing interactions. Bad breath or poor hygiene can be distracting and unpleasant, affecting the other person's comfort and willingness to engage.

Maintaining good personal hygiene shows that you respect yourself and others. It helps in creating a positive and professional image, essential for building strong relationships. Paying attention to personal grooming can enhance your confidence and the quality of your interactions.

BEING DISCONNECTED

Being disconnected from the ongoing conversation or situation can create a barrier to effective communication. This can manifest as appearing uninterested, not participating actively, or failing to respond appropriately. Staying present and engaged in the moment is crucial for meaningful interactions. It shows that you are invested in the conversation and value the relationship. Being connected helps in understanding the other person's perspective and responding thoughtfully.

OVERSHARING

Sharing too much personal information can make the other person uncomfortable and disrupt the professional balance of the conversation. It's important to gauge the appropriateness of the information you share based on the context and the relationship. Keeping conversations professional and relevant helps in maintaining a respectful and comfortable interaction. Oversharing can also divert the conversation away from productive topics. Balancing personal anecdotes with professional insights ensures a healthy conversational flow.

BEING LATE

Punctuality is a sign of respect and reliability. Being late can signal a lack of consideration for the other person's time and can damage your credibility. It sets a negative tone for the interaction and can make the other person feel undervalued. Making an effort to be on time demonstrates your commitment and respect for the relationship. It also helps in building trust and setting a positive foundation for future interactions.

FORGETTING THEIR NAME

Forgetting someone's name is one of the most significant deal breakers in a relationship. It shows a lack of attention and respect for the individual. Remembering and using their name in conversation helps in creating a personal connection and shows that you value them. It's a simple yet powerful way to demonstrate respect and build rapport. Paying attention to names and making an effort to remember them can significantly enhance the quality of your interactions.

STRATEGIES FOR OVERCOMING RELATIONSHIP ISSUES

Open and Honest Communication - Address issues head-on with open and honest communication. Acknowledge mistakes, express your commitment to resolving the issue, and actively listen to the other party's concerns.

Show Empathy -Understanding the perspective and feelings of others can help de-escalate conflicts and foster mutual respect. Show empathy by validating their concerns and demonstrating your willingness to find a solution.

Seek Compromise -Be willing to compromise and find a middle ground. This demonstrates your commitment to the relationship and your willingness to work collaboratively.

Continuous Improvement -Regularly seek feedback and make necessary improvements. Show that you value the relationship by continuously striving to be better and addressing any areas of concern.

5. Build a Culture of Respect - Foster a culture of respect within your organization. Encourage respectful behavior, recognize contributions, and address any instances of disrespect promptly.

ACTIONABLE STEPS FOR ENTREPRENEURS

1. **Prioritize clear and regular communication**: Establish consistent communication channels and encourage open dialogue.

2. **Maintain consistency in your actions and promises**: Build trust by being reliable and following through on commitments.

3. **Show respect in all interactions**: Treat partners, clients, and employees with respect and acknowledge their value.

4. **Balance self-interest with the needs of others**: Foster mutually beneficial relationships by being considerate of others' needs.

5. **Nurture and maintain relationships**: Regularly check in, show appreciation, and address any concerns promptly.

6. **Set and manage expectations**: Be realistic about what you can deliver and communicate openly about any challenges.

7. **Build and maintain trust**: Act with integrity, be transparent, and uphold ethical standards.

8. **Handle conflicts constructively**: Address conflicts directly, seek mutually beneficial solutions, and avoid defensiveness.

9. **Value feedback**: Actively seek and act on feedback

to show that you are committed to continuous improvement.

SUMMARY

Identifying and avoiding relationship killers and deal breakers is essential for maintaining strong, healthy business relationships. By prioritizing clear communication, consistency, respect, and empathy, entrepreneurs can overcome relationship issues and foster a culture of trust and collaboration.

Implementing the strategies and actionable steps outlined in this chapter will help ensure the longevity and success of your business relationships.

CHAPTER NOTES & REMINDERS
YOUR ACTIONABLE GOALS OR PLANS

1.	2.
3.	4.
5.	6.
7.	8.
9.	10.

ILLUSTRATIONS

THANK YOU FOR PURCHASING & READING

Who: Skye Connect Inc is in the consulting industry but also solidifies its reputation as a leader in serving as a National Speaker, Presenter, Keynote Strategist and teacher in strategic innovation and entrepreneurship.

Vision: Our vision is to cultivate an ecosystem where businesses and individuals thrive by taking actionable steps to shape and embrace creativity and excellence through the lens of business and corporate strategies.

Desire: To inspire a new way of thinking for those trail blazers ready to foster innovation and success by em-powering leaders with strategic corporate training, cus-tomized employee assessments and technical development.

Academic: Research papers accepted at the Gulf South Business Research Symposium, the Midwest Academy of Management (MAOM) and the United States Association for Small Business Entrepreneurship (USASBE).

Resources:

Published Scholar:
Google Scholar—Published: Holloway, A. G. (2021). Threading the needle of entrepreneurial orientation of firms: The effects of disruptive threats and turbulence on corporate social responsibility actions and competitiveness (Doctoral dissertation, University of South Alabama).

Presented Paper:
Cheaper, Faster, Better: The Interconnectivity Be-tween Automation, Outsourcing and Organizational Effectiveness"

Industry Experience:
Electric Utility manager with nuclear power operations experience, mass transportation, cities and muncipalities and industry.

Thriving in the business of Entrepreneurship with 4 Steps to Smarter Business Mastery

Find out how to innovate and automate

- **Innovation:** More than new products—it's about smarter value delivery, problem-solving, and efficiency. Identify unmet needs, adapt, and pivot as markets evolve.
- **Automation:** Leverage technology to reduce manual work, boost efficiency, and scale faster. Use AI, CRM systems, and automated workflows to save time and minimize errors.

02
Get comfortable with re-inventing yourself

- Entrepreneurship demands continuous learning and adaptation. Stay open to change, feedback, and new opportunities—shed outdated habits and evolve with the market.

03
Learn how to become an industry disrupter

- Breakthroughs come from challenging the status quo. Disrupt wisely by questioning norms, embracing bold ideas, and taking strategic risks to redefine your industry.

04
Prioritize wellness and lose a few hours of sleep a night (temporarily)

- Health is wealth, but entrepreneurship demands sacrifice. Commit to wellness while accepting that temporary long hours and sleepless nights are part of growth.

BOOK NOW

Need expert insights?

Book a session with Dr. Holloway now!

@ALICETHECONNECT

5 EASY WAYS
TO SELL MORE IN ANY BUSINESS

GRAB NOW!

Topic 1
Understand your customer's life cycle

Topic 2
Offer a 1- week free trial or free product demonstration this column.

Topic 3
Record an unboxing experience

Topic 4
Implement a Custom Relationship Management (CRM) platform to manage customer data (i.e., ZOHO, Salesforce, Microsoft Dynamics, Pipedrive)

Topic 5
Ask customer to record a 10-second testimonial

SUBSCRIBE 🔔

@THEALICECONNECT

WATCH ON YOUTUBE

About the Author
Alice Gordon Holloway, Ph.D.

B lending expertise, technology and kinetic energy, thought leader Dr. Alice Gordon Holloway is an award-winning International Association of Business Communicators corporate strategist well known as a distinguished serial entrepreneur, academic professor and community volunteer renowned for her dynamic approach and innovative mindset.

As a CEO and Founder of Skye Connect Incorporated since 2013, and recently, Skye Connect Transport, Dr. Alice has assisted over 2,200 high impact industry professionals focus on driving organizational and entrepreneurial success across multiple industries. Her mantra, "what gets measured gets done" drives her success as a visionary leader and problem solver.

Additionally, she is active in the classroom teaching the new generation of college students at the University of Alabama as Instructor of Management (Adjunct) where she integrates cutting-edge research with practical insights to shape the next generation of leaders. Her strategic prowess extends to notable collaborations with prominent organizations around the US, working within leaders and managers in organizations and entrepreneurs, along with her focus on research in entrepreneurship and emerging technologies influencing both academia and industry.

Dr. Alice completed her Ph.D. in Business Administration in Management from the University of South Alabama, Master of Business Administration from the University of Alabama at Birmingham and Bachelors' Degree from the University of South Alabama. She consistently freely shares knowledge, strategy tips and interviews on her social engagement channels and YouTube - @theAliceConnect.

To Book, Connect or Schedule A Session with Dr. Holloway, visit –www.draliceholloway.com or email – letstalk@thealiceconnect.com